KU-078-465

Introduction

You are Samuel Pepys (say 'peeps'), born in 1633 and the fifth of eleven children. You're the son of a humble tailor, but through hard work and talent – and help from a rich relative, Sir Edward Montagu – you become Clerk for the Royal Navy for King Charles II of England.

Around 1660, you begin keeping a secret diary, little knowing what horrors lie ahead. In 1665, London is devastated by a deadly plague that kills 100,000 people. Then, in the early hours of 2 September 1666, a fire breaks out in a bakery in the heart of the City. The blaze spreads rapidly. Like everyone else, you're terrified your house and belongings will be destroyed. What can you do to stop the fire spreading, especially when the streets are packed with Londoners desperate to escape the inferno?

The Great Fire of London raged for four nights and days. Most of medieval London was burnt to the ground.

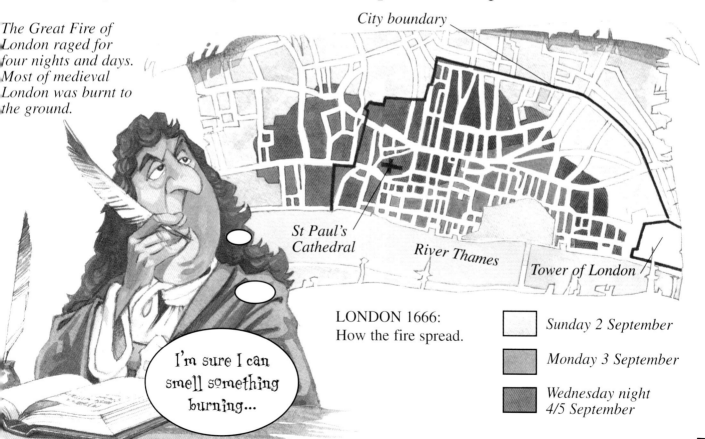

City boundary

St Paul's Cathedral

River Thames

Tower of London

I'm sure I can smell something burning...

LONDON 1666: How the fire spread.

Sunday 2 September

Monday 3 September

Wednesday night 4/5 September

Dirty old town

Strolling through London in the summer of 1666, it's easy to be swamped by the sights, sounds and smells of this busy metropolis. London is a giant city with over 300,000 inhabitants. It's also a centre for trade, finance and government, a wealthy place where lords are carried in grand coaches by servants.

Yet the old centre of London, the City, is a horrible place. Its smoky streets are narrow, stuffy and dark. The summer of 1666 is hot and the place is bone-dry after 10 months of drought. You hold your nose to avoid the stench of dead dogs and rotting waste.

Why is life so grim?

IN THE NOISY STREETS, shouting matches are common. There are no street signs so you find your way around by shop signs. A sign showing a dragon marks an apothecary's (chemist's), and Adam and Eve mark a fruit shop.

FASHION. Women wear hideous white make-up made from poisonous lead. It smells foul and cracks when they smile. People use small bits of mouse skin to make their eyebrows look stylish!

WIGS. Charles II begins wearing wigs when he sees his first grey hairs. Most men copy him. Nits and lice are common problems.

MEDICINE is basic. Hospitals are a place to rest, but little else. Doctors cure their patients using leeches to suck their blood.

Mustn't smile, mustn't smile...

I feel much better, honest!

POLLUTION. Ashes and dust are constantly thrown into the streets. Piles of steaming dung lie everywhere. Every home has a cesspit for sewage. In your diary you moan that your neighbour's cesspit has flooded your cellar.

Troubled times

Even in 21st-century London, it is said that you are never more than 2 metres away from a rat!

I t isn't just the hot weather that bothers you. England is still recovering from a bloody civil war fought between Parliament and King Charles I. In 1660, King Charles II was restored to the throne, but old rivalries remain.

A year ago, a third of Londoners died during a horrific plague. The churchyards were full of bodies piled on top of each other. The plague has almost died out now, but death carts still rattle around the streets. To make matters worse, England is at war with the Netherlands, and there is tension between Protestants and Catholics.

Where are we going to bury them all?

Why are people so fearful?

PLAGUE. In September 1665, the plague killed 8,000 Londoners in a single week. In October, the disease died down, as cold weather killed rats carrying the infected fleas that cause the disease. But 100,000 Londoners were already dead.

TENSION. London is a largely Protestant place. In 1605 a group of Catholics led by Guy Fawkes tried to blow up Parliament – the Gunpowder Plot. Protestants now fear another Catholic plot to destroy the city.

Handy hint

Your wig might be made from the hair of a person who was infected by the plague, so don't wear it. Better to be untrendy than dead!

WAR. In recent times England has been at war with Spain and France and in September 1666 it is fighting the Dutch. Londoners are suspicious of foreigners, especially the French, as they fear a French invasion.

Pepys' diary describes the plague. Houses with victims were marked with a red cross and were guarded so no-one could escape. By June 1665 the roads were clogged with people fleeing London.

Never trust a man with a French hat!

FLOODED & FROZEN. In 1663, high tide flooded central London. The River Thames also froze over for several winters in the 1660s. At the best of times, the river is full of floating corpses and waste. At low tide it stinks horribly.

9

A bonfire waiting to happen?

I'll be toast if I hang around here any longer!

People cook and heat their houses with open *and use candles in the dark. Some smoke in b or sweep hot ashes under the stairs.*

As if Londoners don't already have enough worries, fires are common. A fire in 1633 burnt for 8 hours and wrecked over 80 houses. Despite this, open fires burn in houses, shops and workshops. Craftsmen light braziers in the streets. The houses crowded inside the City walls are built of timber. Straw is laid on floors and stored in stables, so a careless neighbour can soon start a mighty blaze.

You've heard all sorts of predictions that London will burn down. Being a superstitious chap, you wear a hare's foot around your neck as a good-luck charm. Terrifyingly, your worst fears are about to come true.

Who predicts the Great Fire?

IN APRIL 1665, Charles II warns the Lord Mayor of the fire risks of the City's wooden houses and narrow streets. From 1600 to 1665 there have been at least 70 big fires in English towns.

SUPERSTITIOUS PEOPLE believe they see signs of disaster. At Easter it rains fish in Kent. In July, egg-sized hailstones fall in Norfolk. Months before the fire, the Spanish ambassador says he sees a monster 'with a human face, the legs of a bull, the tail of a wolf and the breast of a goat'.

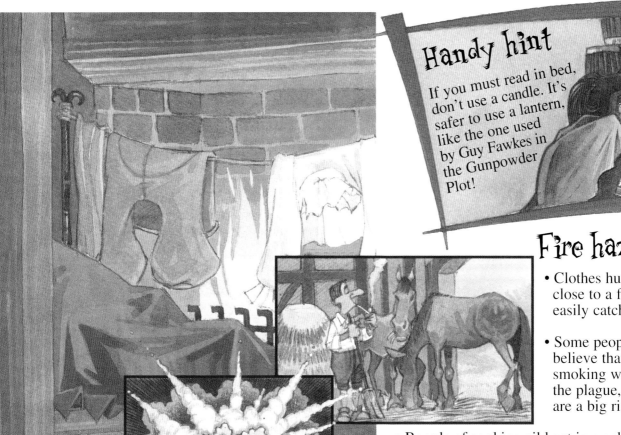

Handy hint

If you must read in bed, don't use a candle. It's safer to use a lantern, like the one used by Guy Fawkes in the Gunpowder Plot!

Fire hazard!

- Clothes hung too close to a fire can easily catch alight.

- Some people believe that smoking wards off the plague, so fires are a big risk.

- Barrels of cooking oil kept in a cellar can create a raging inferno if they catch fire.

- In 1649, 27 barrels of gunpowder stored in a cellar blew up, destroying 41 houses and killing 67 people.

RELIGIOUS PAMPHLETS have been warning of a great fire for years. They say that God is going to send fire to punish Londoners for their sins. You're afraid bad things may happen in 1666 because 666 is the symbol of the devil.

IN A BOOK written in 1641, Mother Shipton, a so-called witch from York, predicts that 'London in '66 should be burnt to ashes'. People take such warnings very seriously.

May the fires of hell rain down on London!

Mother Shipton says things are hotting up!

11

The fire begins

Saturday 1 September is another hot, dry day. Trade is busy and by closing time, baker Tom Farynor is exhausted. When he cools the ovens, he misses a glowing ember.

While you are sleeping in the early hours of Sunday 2 September, a small fire starts in Farynor's bakery on Pudding Lane. It is fanned by the easterly breeze blowing across the city. The fire spreads quickly through the house. Soon after 2 a.m., Farynor's assistant is woken by thick smoke. He raises the alarm and Farynor and his family escape through an attic window to a neighbour's house – all except a maid, who is scared of heights and stays behind. She is the fire's first victim.

How does the fire spread?

1. FARYNOR'S BAKERY. As Farynor's bakery burns, a group from the nearby Star Inn stand and gawp, rather than trying to put out the fire.

Farynor's neighbour even has time to remove his goods before the fire spreads to his house. Then, without warning, the roof of the bakery suddenly collapses.

2. STAR INN. Sparks blow across the yard to the Star Inn, which instantly catches fire. The flames are soon roaring. People living in Pudding Lane and Fish Street Hill pour onto the streets to put out the flames.

Handy hint

Take the fire seriously! When the Lord Mayor is woken and told of the fire, he says: 'Pish, a woman could put the fire out by peeing on it!' and goes back to bed.

4. THE RIVERSIDE WAREHOUSES are packed with oil, pitch, hay, coal, hemp and tar. These fuel the fire, which burns so fiercely that no-one can get close enough to fight the flames.

5. THE CITY. The strong wind spreads the flames into the City. By 8 a.m., the blaze has spread halfway across London Bridge, destroying the houses that are built on the bridge itself. Luckily, a gap in the houses created by the fire of 1633 stops it spreading across the river.

Pudding Lane

Fish Street Hill

London Bridge

Thames Street

It's hotter than the devil's underwear.

The yellow area (above) shows how far the fire spread on Sunday 2 September

3. THAMES STREET. Sparks carried by the strong east wind set alight wooden houses up to 200 metres away. Timber beams fall across the streets and provide another route for the fire. Towards dawn, the fire spreads to St Botolph's Lane and down Fish Street Hill to the warehouses on Thames Street.

The blaze spreads

A couple of hours after the blaze starts, your maid wakes you to warn of the danger. Seeing the fire is some way off, you head back to bed. She bursts in later with news that 300 buildings are already in ashes. This is no ordinary blaze. You hurry to the top of the Tower of London to see for yourself. Getting into a boat, you watch burning timbers fall into the water – the river itself seems on fire! The blaze is spreading west at great speed, whipped along by the wind. Around 11 a.m., you travel to Whitehall to tell the King.

How do people react?

HOLDING OUT. People stay in their homes as long as they can. You see pigeons unwilling to leave their nests, hovering above the flaming roofs until their wings burn and they fall into the fire.

WHAT FIRE? It's a while before people realise the danger. Swedish diplomat Francisco de Rapicani describes having lunch out with friends. They return home to find 'their houses have gone up in fire and smoke'!

FIREBREAKS. By the time the Lord Mayor arrives, the fire has spread to the river. One way of stopping it is to create firebreaks by pulling down houses in its path. But when the owners refuse to let him demolish their homes, the Mayor hesitates. Quick action could have stopped the fire from spreading.

Forget it!

Please! Let me pull down your house!

14

Everything will burn, even the churches! I must tell the King!*

Handy hint

If you're making a run for it, don't forget your pet! Later in the week you see a shivering cat. Its fur has been burnt off by the flames but it is still alive.

PANIC. By now everyone is fleeing, pushing their way through narrow streets. People and horses are running over each other! It's very hard to get water pumps (see page 16) to the fire quickly.

He's got a firebomb!

It's just a tennis ball!

ANGER. On the way to see the King, you meet an angry crowd who believe God has sent the fire. There's also a rumour that foreigners are throwing fireballs to start the fires. Mobs, armed with clubs and home-made weapons, attack anyone who can't speak good English.

Despite what Pepys had seen, he still had a dinner party for his friends that night!

Battling the inferno

When you tell the King the bad news, he leaps into action. A coach takes you to the Lord Mayor with orders that no houses are to be spared in putting out the fire. By noon a few firebreaks have been created, but they're too close to the fire to stop it. That afternoon, the King lends a hand to the people fighting the fire. By now the flames are shooting 30 metres into the air. Later that night, you watch from the river. Your face is burned by a shower of 'fire drops'.

How can the fire be stopped?

That's more like it!

I'm too tired to care! I need more men!

FIRE BRIGADE? There isn't one. Locals fight the flames with water carried in leather buckets or by beating the fire out. The authorities have a few hand-pumped machines that squirt water, but they won't stop fast-moving fires.

Water pump

ASK THE MAYOR? Don't bother. When you finally deliver the King's message to the Lord Mayor he drops to his knees, whimpering.

On Tuesday night, soldiers and sailors use gunpowder to knock down houses, which proves far more effective.

BOOM!

Handy hint

By Sunday evening the fire is so strong it's moving against the wind – toward your house! Go home and pack up your belongings!

Those wigs must be soundproofed!

PULL HOMES DOWN? Where fires threaten to spread, people use axes, ropes and iron fire hooks to drag down buildings and create firebreaks. But the wind sweeps the fire so fast that the houses can't be pulled down quickly enough. At its peak, the blaze wrecks about 100 houses an hour.

WATER PUMPS? There's a system of wooden water pipes below ground to feed the pumps during fires. In the rush to stop the fire, people tear up the streets, piercing the pipes in so many places that there is no pressure to squirt the water out.

Uh-oh!

17

A lake of fire

How can you save your belongings?

At 4 a.m. the next day, Monday, you move your silver and valuables to a friend's house outside the City walls. You're in such a rush you don't change out of your nightgown!

Meanwhile, the Royal Exchange building, packed with expensive silks and spices, goes up in flames. The smoke turns the sky red.

On Tuesday, the fire moves west and north. After midnight, it destroys the Guildhall and St Paul's Cathedral. Lead melted from buildings runs down streets that are glowing with the heat. Around 2 a.m. on Wednesday your wife wakes you. The fire is perilously close to your house. You decide to escape by boat.

BY RIVER. You pay £8 for two boats to carry your furniture downriver to Deptford. Other people flee in 'wherries' – small river boats. You see a few boats carrying virginals (musical instruments). The Thames is littered with abandoned goods.

BY CART. When the river boats are filled with refugees, there's only one way for people to move their things – by cart. The price of a cart rises from £3 to £30 in two days. One desperate man even pays £400 (around £40,000 today).

£400?

It's my hottest price!

ON FOOT. Some people can't afford boats, so they carry what they can. Sick and elderly people will need a helping hand. With London Bridge in flames there's no way across the river except by boat. Few people know how to swim.

UNDERGROUND. People with valuables bury or hide them underground before fleeing. On Tuesday you bury your prized Parmesan cheeses and wine stores. You also place some important documents in your neighbour's pit.

The fire dies down

Pepys was very sad to see the smoking ruins of St Paul's Cathedral.

The fire rages for four nights and days. You see houses in the east being blown up by gunpowder, which creates large firebreaks and saves the Tower of London. But in the west, the fire leaps across the Fleet River and threatens Whitehall and the royal palaces.

Finally, on Wednesday morning, the wind drops. The fire slowly begins to burn out. At last people can put out the flames, though they battle for another 36 hours before the last fires are extinguished on Thursday night. Earlier that day you walk around the smoking ruins of the City. Small fires smoulder for many weeks after.

Why did the fire stop?

WIND. The east wind fanned the fire. When it dropped the flames died down.

STONE WALLS. The Temple is an ancient medieval church surrounded by stone buildings belonging to lawyers. Finally the fire had come up against buildings it couldn't burn.

DEMOLITION. On Monday the King asked the Duke of York (the future James II) to take charge. The Duke organised a series of explosions that stopped the fire.

What about the survivors?

OVER 100,000 Londoners have had to flee their homes. Many go to the suburbs and stay there. Some go to other towns, while others emigrate to America. In the winter of 1666, the fields around London are full of the homeless living in tents.

Navy biscuit – hard biscuits used by the Navy – is handed out but many people refuse it.

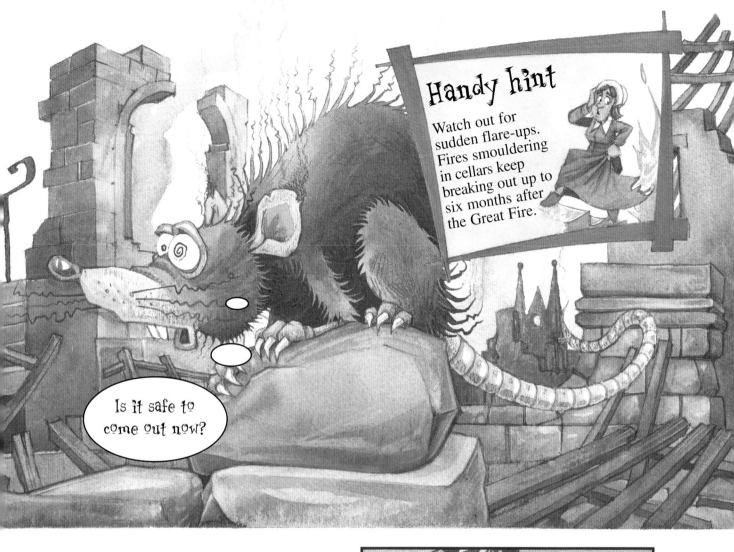

Watch out for sudden flare-ups. Fires smouldering in cellars keep breaking out up to six months after the Great Fire.

Is it safe to come out now?

SHACKED UP. Some Londoners set up shacks made from charred wood and fallen bricks over the smoking rubble. This is brave but very dangerous. At night many people are robbed, murdered and then buried in the ruins.

ROASTED. Not everyone was able to escape the flames. Londoner Thomas Taswell describes his horror at finding the gruesome remains of an old woman burnt in the fire.

21

A city in ruins

You're incredibly lucky – the fire stops at the end of your street, Seething Lane, and your house is untouched. Because your house is a government building, you persuaded the Duke of York to create firebreaks nearby to protect your street! But all around there is devastation. The Great Fire is one of the greatest disasters in London's history. Thousands of people have lost their homes, businesses and belongings.

News of the Great Fire quickly spreads around Europe and foreign newspapers print the story with dramatic drawings of the fire.

DESTRUCTION. The Great Fire has destroyed 13,200 houses and four-fifths of the City of London, including the Royal Exchange and the Custom House. As well as St Paul's Cathedral, 87 churches are destroyed.

St Paul's Cathedral

River Thames

LOST LIVES. The Great Fire starts slowly, so there is plenty of time for people to save themselves. Officially, there are just five deaths: Thomas Farynor's maid; Paul Lowell, a watchmaker; an old man who was overcome by smoke; and two others who fell into their cellars while rescuing their belongings.

BANKRUPTCY.
So many merchants are ruined that a new prison is built for those who can't pay their debts. Others kill themselves. After the fire, Sarah Crofts, once a wealthy woman, has to work as a servant after losing property worth £5,000.

Handy hint

Even if your house is burnt, check your cellar for any goods that aren't ruined. The Grocers' Company found 100 kg of silver from coins that had melted in the heat!

Tower of London

Royal Exchange

Southwark

London Bridge

Who's to blame?

During the Great Fire many post offices and newspaper offices are burnt down, so there is little reliable news. Instead, rumours spread that the fire is an attack by the French or Dutch. Mobs roam the streets, attacking anyone they suspect. To calm things down, King Charles speaks to refugees at Moorfields.

He tells them the fire was simply an accident, but most still people believe the fire was started deliberately. On 25 September 1666, Parliament sets up an official inquiry. Frenchman Robert Hubert is hanged for starting the fire. But a year later, the King's Council agrees the fire was an accident, helped by the dry summer, the strong wind and the wooden houses.

Whodunnit?

CHARLES II? Some whisper that Charles II (below) started the fire to distract from scandals at court. The 'Merry Monarch' is not as popular as he once was, thanks to badly behaved courtiers. But it's unlikely the King is to blame, as he lost a lot of money in the blaze.

A FRENCHMAN? Confused watchmaker Robert Hubert (right) confesses to starting the fire in Westminster, even though he wasn't in London until two days after it started! The jury probably knows he is innocent but everyone is keen to point the finger. Poor Hubert is hanged on 27 October 1666.

CATHOLICS? When the official inquiry publishes its first report, it includes rumours that Catholics started the fire. Many Londoners are willing to believe these made-up stories.

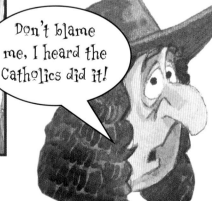

Don't blame me, I heard the Catholics did it!

LORD MAYOR? Just two years earlier, Charles II wrote to the Lord Mayor (left) asking him to encourage builders to use brick rather than wood. If the mayor had only followed the King's advice, the fire might not have spread as far or as quickly as it did.

Handy hint

If you're a foreigner, stay at home. It's probably best if you don't talk to anyone until everything calms down!

Cornelius Riedtveldt, a Dutch baker from Westminster, is attacked by a mob and his bakery looted. He is nearly beaten to death.

You've got the wrong baker!

THE BAKER?
In court, Thomas Farynor
(left) flatly denies that the fire started in his bakery.
Meanwhile, Farynor and two other members of his
family are on the jury that finds Hubert guilty!

Rebuilding London

After the fire, there's lots to be done. Troops are put on alert in case there's a French invasion. The streets are cleared and new markets are created so everyone can get back to business. People also argue about how the City should be rebuilt. Some want a modern, elegant city with wider streets and fireproof houses.

Throughout 1667, people clear rubble and survey the burnt area. New laws are passed on how houses should be built. But by the end of the year just 150 new houses are finished. For decades, parts of the City lie in ruins. The rebuilding lasts for nearly 50 years. The new St Paul's Cathedral is only completed in 1710.

Looks like a sure-fire winner to me!

A SUM OF £16, 201 is raised to help victims of the Great Fire, but it doesn't really compare with the £10 million lost in the blaze! King Charles II wants to show that London is a great city, so public buildings are paid for by a new tax on coal. The Guildhall, Customs House, Royal Exchange, prisons, as well as churches and St Paul's Cathedral, are all rebuilt.

BY 1671, some 9,000 houses are rebuilt, most in brick instead of wood. City streets, like Fleet Street, are widened and new streets are created. Pavements are built for the first time and new sewers are added. By 1672, most of those who lost houses have new homes.

The new streets look good!

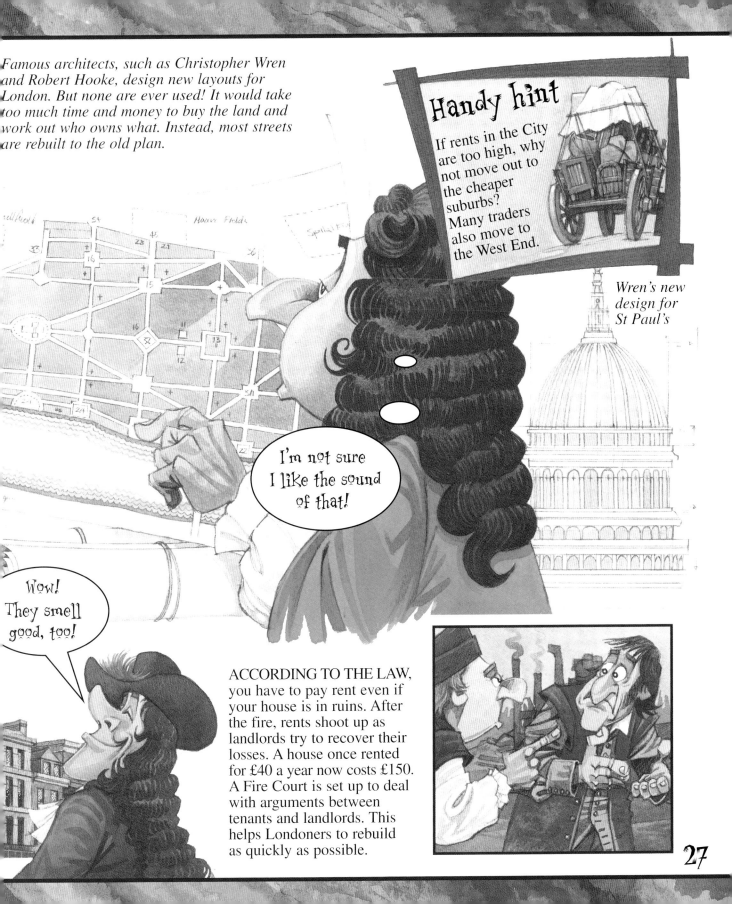

Famous architects, such as Christopher Wren and Robert Hooke, design new layouts for London. But none are ever used! It would take too much time and money to buy the land and work out who owns what. Instead, most streets are rebuilt to the old plan.

Handy hint

If rents in the City are too high, why not move out to the cheaper suburbs? Many traders also move to the West End.

Wren's new design for St Paul's

I'm not sure I like the sound of that!

Wow! They smell good, too!

ACCORDING TO THE LAW, you have to pay rent even if your house is in ruins. After the fire, rents shoot up as landlords try to recover their losses. A house once rented for £40 a year now costs £150. A Fire Court is set up to deal with arguments between tenants and landlords. This helps Londoners to rebuild as quickly as possible.

27

Aftermath

The Great Fire is a disaster but it does bring change. Many of the new houses are built in brick and stone. A huge army of migrant workers come to rebuild the city, along with craftsmen to furnish the new houses. By the early 18th century, London is the largest city in Europe and probably the richest. It also has some wonderful new buildings, such as St Paul's.

Though houses built after the Great Fire are safer, a large fire in 1676 destroys over 600 houses south of the river. In January 1673, a fire destroys your home. Eleven years later another home of yours is only saved when a neighbour's house is blown up to create a firebreak. Will you ever be able to sleep in peace?

Better firefighting

INSURANCE. There is no home insurance so Londoners have to pay for their burnt houses to be rebuilt. This is such a problem that in 1680 Nicholas Barbon sets up the first insurance company, called The Fire Office. However, London doesn't have a proper fire brigade until 1866.

A NEW LAW passed in 1668 requires Londoners to keep a better look-out for fires. Large numbers of buckets, ladders and pick-axes are kept at the ready.

Oh, not again!

FIRE ENGINE. In the 1670s, Dutch inventor Jan van der Heyden invents a new fire engine with a leather hose known as a 'worm' or 'snake'. It also has an air pump that creates a continuous stream of water. The fire engine is first used in London in the 1690s.

The Monument

Handy hint

Look out for the yellow flowers of wild mustard that grow over the wastelands created by the fire. The flowers spread so fast that they are nicknamed 'London rocket'!

What survives today?

BURNT. Very few buildings from before the fire still stand today, though some survived into the 19th century.

THE GEORGE

St Paul's Cathedral

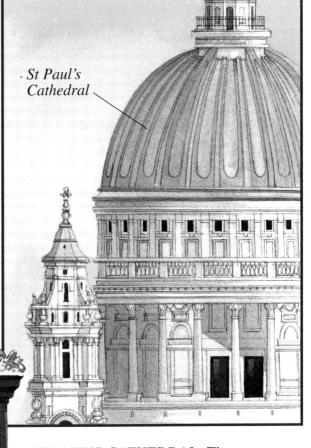

THE MONUMENT. Designed by Wren and Hooke, this column (right) marks the Great Fire. It stands near Pudding Lane, close to where the fire started. It's 62 m tall. You can still climb the column's 311 interior steps to enjoy the view from the top.

ST PAUL'S CATHEDRAL. The most famous building designed by Wren, the new cathedral was built from 1675 to 1710. Twenty-nine of the other 51 churches designed by Wren are still standing.

Glossary

Apothecary A historical name for a chemist or pharmacist.

Bankrupt Having no money and unable to pay one's debts.

Brazier A large metal container in which coal or charcoal was burned, used to warm people.

Cesspit A large pit dug into the ground, used to collect sewage or rubbish in the days before towns had sewers.

Chamber pot A bowl-shaped pot with a handle, kept in the bedroom under a bed or in a cabinet, used for going to the toilet in the night. Also known as a bedpan.

Civil War The war fought between the supporters of Parliament, led by Oliver Cromwell, and King Charles I. It lasted from 1641 to 1651. It ended with the Parliamentary victory at the Battle of Worcester on 3 September 1651.

Clerk Pepys' full title was Clerk of the Acts. He was responsible for organising supplies for the Royal Navy.

Coal tax After the Great Fire of London, Parliament introduced a tax on coal which it used to rebuild the city.

Courtier Someone who attends the court of a king or queen. In the past, the court was a centre of power and courtiers who flattered the king might be rewarded with money, land or titles.

Drought A long dry spell of weather, often leading to a shortage of water.

Ember A hot fragment of wood or coal left from a fire that is still glowing or smouldering.

Fireball A ball of animal fat, called tallow, set alight and used to start fires.

Firebreak A gap between houses that stops a fire from spreading. During the Great Fire, firebreaks were created by pulling down houses or blowing them up.

Fire Court A special court set up after the Great Fire to settle arguments between landlords and tenants.

Hemp A fibre made from the hemp plant that was used in the past to make ropes and nets.

Inquiry An official investigation.

Insurance An agreement that protects against a future loss. For example, if you insure a house and it burns down, you will be paid the money to rebuild it.

King's Council A group of ministers who helped advise the king.

Leech A bloodsucking worm-like creature that often lives in water. In the past, leeches were used to draw blood from patients as a supposed cure for many different illnesses and diseases.

Lord Mayor The elected head of the City of London's governing body.

Metropolis A large and heavily populated city, such as London.

Migrant Someone who comes to live in a different country.

Navy biscuit A hard biscuit made of flour, salt and water used by the Royal Navy to feed crews on long sea voyages.

Parliament The government of England which passes new laws.

Pitch A black, sticky substance, also known as tar, that is used to stop wooden ships from leaking.

Plague A deadly disease spread quickly by fleas.

River Fleet A small river than flows south into the River Thames in London.

Smoulder To burn without a flame.

Suburb A district lying in the outer parts of a city.

Warehouse A store for goods and merchandise.

Wherry A small boat used to transport goods along a river.

Index